Coming Out With It

6/2/93
To Jenny,
love and best wishes
Angela.

Coming Out With It

Angela McSeveney

Angela McSeveney

From Cliches → Ponytail, the poems are in chronological order; Cliches was written when I was 19, Ponytail when I was 28. The 'Just Domestic' Poems were written when I was 27; Polygon asked if they could be printed first as they were a "strong way" to start.

Polygon
EDINBURGH

© Angela McSeveney 1992

Published by Polygon
22 George Square
Edinburgh

Set in Linotron Sabon
by Koinonia, Bury and
printed and bound in
Great Britain by
Redwood Press Ltd.,
Melksham, Wiltshire.

British Library Cataloguing in
    Publication Data
McSeveney, Angela
    Coming Out With It
    I. Title
    821. 914

ISBN 0 7486 6137 9

The Publisher acknowledges
subsidy from the Scottish Arts
Council towards the publication
of this volume.

CONTENTS

ACKNOWLEDGEMENTS

I would like to thank the following people:

the editors of all the magazines which have printed my poetry in the past: *Ambit, Chapman, The Echo Room, Edinburgh Review, Envoi 85, Fox, Graffitti, The Jacaranda Review, London Magazine, The Other Merry Go Round, Pause, The Pen, Pennine Platform, Poetry Nottingham, Staple 7, Verse, Weyfarers, The White Rose Magazine, Writing*;

the editors of *Original Prints*, Volumes 2 and 3, and Robert Crawford who edited *Other Tongues*;

the following writers-in-residence at Edinburgh University – Ron Butlin, Liz Lochhead and Alan Spence;

some of my teachers – Katherine Awlson, Alexander Beaton and Dr Cairns Craig

and finally, The Scottish Arts Council Bursary Panel.

THE JUST DOMESTIC POEMS

Changing a Downie Cover
Starching a Linen Blouse
Blacking a Hearth Stone

CHANGING A DOWNIE COVER

First: catch your downie.

They're big animals, sleep a lot of the time,
barely stirring as they snooze endlessly
loafing around on the beds.

But they only have to see
a clean cover –

suddenly you have six by three
of feathery incorporeality kicking and screaming
in your hands.

Wrestle them to the floor
and kneel on their necks:
you can't hurt them, no bones to break.

Pushing their head into the bag
keeps them quiet

but you're never sure
till each corner is flush inside the cover
securely buttoned shut.

They give up after that.
Pinioned in floral print polycotton
they lie back down and sleep.

STARCHING A LINEN BLOUSE

The blouse finds its backbone
begins to fill out
take shape.

Each sleeve peels from the sticky board
with a sound like sellotape
tearing off the roll.

When I button it onto a hanger
it holds its own arms out
like a patient child being dressed.

With its linen pectorals flung out
it hangs to attention
like a stuffed shirt.

BLACKING A HEARTH STONE

I kneel
with the floor as an easel,

clean up my dull grey canves
with a duster and a wet cloth,

I work with just one pigment
charcoal dark.

Back bent with patience
I smooth it on with my fingertips
kneading at the pitted rock.

On rougher parts I work close
with an old nailbrush.

Later it dries
and I buff on a varnished shine
with a soft cloth.

I straighten up, stand back,
admire my Study In Black
framed by an armchair and a pale rug.

CLICHÉS

Once upon a time I uttered words
as meaningless as myself.

They could only be approximations
and always of someone else's feelings

but Autumn leaves do look like carpet on the ground
and hearts can at least come close to breaking.

EXPOSURE

He tore half my torso from me when he left.

My nerve-endings hung invisible in the air.
Old associations sharpened their awareness
but only to pain.

Stunned they danced in their anguish
then curled back inside my wounds.

ROOM-MATES

You are the body in the other bed.
You read magazines I never buy
and leave your toothpaste next to mine.

I know you have a boyfriend
but you take the pill without water
at the corner of my eye.

Modest I shuffle beneath my nightdress
and hide myself from your small breasts.

That tree is black now
and blends with the bricks behind it.

No-one else noticed the gradual decay
of winter settle onto it
nor even now the silent hope of uncurled buds.

I watched it through the last days
of Autumn; saw it rattled in the wind.

Always it seemed glazed in gold,
as in November.

Then it was radiant and I was too.

MIST ON THE MEADOWS

Seagulls stand grounded in the wet and peck,
bored, at surfacing worms.

Vision ends at twenty yards.
Somewhere traffic makes the ground tremble.

I can see smudged trees
if I look hard.

Someone throws something to an invisible dog.

Breathing nears me
then jogs past, red and sweating.

MY CRIME

Unlike my brother I did not die young.

I had fits and croup, caused sleepless nights
and trips to clinics.

My feet outgrew shoes which cost money
and I was no beauty.

I answered back, stayed out and was ungrateful.
People washed their hands of me (more than once).

Unlike me my brother died young
golden haired, one week old, in an incubator.

EDINBURGH SUBURB

Striding along your wide paved elegance
I wear no tights and one shoe flaps unbuckled.

I cast an appraising eye
at your privet hedges and pink and white cherry trees
now bent with blossom.

I arrived via my comprehensive education
and damp fairy tale cottages
built into damper embankments.

Once my princesses lived here.
They wore pale blue party dresses, buckled shoes
and silver christening bracelets.

SUNBATHING

Sunshine came and lay beside me on my towel.
Rolling over, he pressed a warm belly flat against
                                                    mine.

Yellow warmth hung on the curves of my haunches.
Sunshine rubbed his brow in the crook of my arm.

Blood red, I stayed behind my eyelids.
Opening them, I gazed at china plate blue.

Oriental style, one branch of blossom grew from a
                                                    corner.
Sunshine held my face between his warm hands.

My breasts
walk ahead of me.

They collect crumbs and bruises.
Dripping coffee makes them wince.

Pallid as flour sacks
they sag from their lace-trimmed harness
and take up my lap like twin babes.

Roll over in the night
and they spill into my arms.
I can curl myself around them
alone in the dark.

Their imagination moves them.

The nipples stir in search
of a sucking mouth.

Or tense with expectation
they lean against my ribcage
and wait.

I left home this Summer
two years after I moved away.

No one heard me say goodbye
but my roots came up bloodstained.

KIRSTY

The radio reports the disappearance
of a seven year-old wearing a blue
quilted jacket and brown lacing shoes.

My stomach clenches
as it did thirteen years before
on an empty building site.

The cement bag spread beneath me
stuck to my back.

RETREAT

Turning the spotlight in on myself
didn't show up any red-eyed demons
I could have put to flight.

There was only me.

I lay beside me in bed.
I read books over my own shoulder.

I would have liked to have opened the door
and shown myself out.

But I wasn't going anywhere.

FOR THE BEST

I don't doubt you did it for the best.

After all I was twenty –
about time somebody did.

One of us was old enough to be my father,
the other to have known better.

I never said the word frigidity
 – only went cold with the fear of it.

You rubbed me up the wrong way
and knowing that I must make the best of it.

COLIN

Colin presided at my first tutorial,
read sex into all the symbolism,
told the tutor where to get off.

He wore striped trousers and pied shirts,
spoke of love being made in the room next to his.

To catch his glance made me blush.

We shared classes again in our second last term.
I wore pink dungarees at the front of the class.

Colin sat behind me in a herringbone coat
and took Jane Austen very seriously indeed.

THE SWEEP

I heard him singing first at the back of my mind.
My bowed head went on working.

When I did raise my tiring eyes they met his
six storeys up across the way.

Behind the windowpane I drew a breath.
He stepped from one chimney stack to the next
and went on singing.

CROCKERY

My mother stood her potplants on old saucers,
all of them survivors from separate sets.

Each item had been packed into a tea-chest at least
                                    once
then laid out on another shelf.

I remember playing among the balled-up newspaper
on a different kitchen floor.

My mother tended to her red geraniums
and wondered at the crockery
we must have gone through.

She was tall enough for me to love
and I was too lonely to brush her arm aside
when it encircled me.

I saw a wealth of comfort in her figure –
flat enough to feel quite like the few male torsos
I had ever leaned against.

I watched her scan the crowd before she found me
a head's height below her eyes
and I smiled back shyly.

STRETCH MARKS

My growing pains weren't physical.
I didn't feel the push and pull
of my lengthening skeleton

but the white lines show
where my skin took the strain

and the mole on my breast
once lay flat against my ribs.

THE FAT NYMPHOMANIAC'S POEM

Tall men turn me on.
An immense man makes me petite and feminine.

For him I'm so much less the cow in a china shop.
My rugby tackle won't send him flying.

If there's more of him pound for pound
I can lay me down not smothering anyone.

THE LUMP

Rolling over in a hot June night
I cradled my breasts in my arms
and felt a hard knot of tissue.

I was fifteen.
My life rose up in my throat
and threatened to stifle me.

It took three attempts to tell my mother.
She promised that my appointment would be
with a woman doctor.

A nurse called my name.
I didn't have cancer.

The stitches in my skin reminded me
of a chicken trussed for the oven.

I felt ashamed
that the first man to see me
had only been doing his job.

A NEW HOUSE

This place is a clean slate.

Life is as unmarked
as the fresh paint.

I'm using a blank piece of paper
for my next chapter.

Stepping into virgin snow
I've yet to put a foot wrong.

CRYING OUT

It wasn't my voice.

It was my mother,
my sister, the girl I'd once heard
from the room next door.

My mouth was full of their voices,
filled with my surprise.

I became a heavy breathing harmony
for background music.

This couldn't be my voice
for I'd never heard it speak before.

I cried out
full of laughter and surprise.

PREGNANCY

left a maze of scars
on my mother's belly.

Eighty-nine months saw her carry children.
Three years gave back only corpses
for her trauchle.

Once she bared her midriff and showed me
the white line which had gaped
to let me leave her.

A SHALLOW BATH

Lying flat, my belly and breasts still
reach up above the water.

In the steamy primeval mist
my contours become continents.

I watch the cooling flesh dimple,
the nipples crinkle and rise.
As the waters fall away I chart the lie
of this land.

My brimming navel is an oasis.

Flattened hairs lie around like seaweed
then raise their drying heads
like curious vegetation.

TELEPHONE TALKS

I need only call
and you all come running.

I'm the hole in the wall
where Pyramus and Thisbe speak.

With one of you at either ear
I have a share in all your secrets.

Your words are in the balance.
My time is precious, make each minute count.

EXTRA-MURAL CLASS AT THE ART GALLERY

A bud had blossomed.

Dust fell from my dead essays.
I was a Byzantine.
I loved these icons.

Colour bloomed in the Virgin's smile.
Her plump infant gurgled.

The canvases warmed and opened out for me.
Landscapes sang with praise
for their own rich pigments.

A haystack in a snowstorm dazzled me.

OLD FLAME

He was a fever under my skin.
Each night saw me tossed in it.

My heated eyes looked out at the dark
like red-rimmed coals on a pyre.

I was a bush burning on an arid plain.

Yet there never seemed any less flesh on my bones,
any less fuel to feed those flames.

NIGHT SHIFT

I would wake up when I heard Dad
coming in at the front door.

The others slept through his early morning noises:
a toilet flush, one cup of tea boiling.

There seemed no place for him
at home all day Saturday
and most of Sunday.

His skin paled
apart from one weather-beaten patch
at his throat.

'It's no life for a man,' he sometimes grumbled
'this living like a mole.'

During school holidays I made
no noise at home.

Mum went to parents' nights alone.
She was sick of darning where industrial acid
ate away his clothes.

At five o'clock I'd be sent
to waken Dad for tea.

The curtains in my parents' room
were almost always closed.

DASHED HOPES

His goodbye hug was the first time
anyone had volunteered
to touch me.

His brown checked shirt smelled of sweat.
He stroked my hair just once.

Shaking like a leaf
I spun out five seconds
to last a lifetime if they had to.

It felt as intimate as making love.

A long time later
I cried very hard.

I hadn't known that poems speaking
of a lover's heart-beat
simply state the truth.

BETWEEN FRIENDS

He said it might happen again
but really it was just for the moment
between friends.

We didn't let our other flatmates hear.
At one am we sat still
as someone came home late.

He kissed no further than my breasts
and whispered his fears of losing me
as a friend.

Around three o'clock he threw me gently
from his room.

I washed away the dampness
where my body had waited for his.

ULTRASONIC SCAN

In a standard issue one-size shift
I present myself as a votive offering.

I am laid out
and warm oil poured
across my body.

Cold metal skims along my skin
and makes invisible incisions.

I can't read the omens
as my insides flicker
on a black screen.

while he was away

the most shameful thing I did
was rifling through his open mail and envying
letters even his family had signed with love

(the silliest thing
was holding a mirror above my face
then kissing it)

the cruellest was sitting
in his room alone
talking to the space
he ought to fill

it was a thorn in my flesh
that all the films I saw had lovers

I rested my breasts in my arms
they missed him most of all

UNEMPLOYED

When the door slams for the fourth time
my hasty goodbye hangs unheard
at the ceiling.

That last pair of feet is running late
to a nine o'clock deadline.

I too rose early.
'How did your day go?' dares me
to have an unrehearsed reply.

I annoy myself by feeling abused
when I agree to wait in for tradesmen.

I eat lunch alone
staring at the draining board.

As I rinse my cup and plate
the unwashed breakfast dishes watch me.

Perhaps mothers feel like this, minimising the mess
with yesterday's cold vegetables.

A HIRSUTE WOMAN

A friend first mentioned it, not quite
behind her back.

When she filched her father's razor
the bathroom felt as cold
as her dread of discovery.

In Summer she wears long sleeves
and dark tights.

Sometimes she swims alone
and imagines that the flattened hair
looks like fur.

'I'm unemployed.'

That phrase just erased me.
Her reply falls flat.

She daren't ask me if I enjoy it
nor suggest that it must be fun.

I feel like a bluebottle in the ointment.
She brought no prearranged pigeonholes
which can take me.

All she knows is that I do nothing.

'What would you like to do?' she tries,
to fill in my wavering outline.

COMING OUT WITH IT

You couldn't know that I wanted you
so you chose your moment carefully.
I froze.

I took some time to react,
trying to be tactful.

You were frozen too
in my five second pause.

There was sense in your caution.

I was shocked when you told me
about shouts in the street
and your sister's reaction.

But even now for a moment
homosexual stops being a trait.
It rears up, a title.

I blink it away.
You settle into focus.

You say that when you told me
I stopped stroking your hand.

I smile because you still can't measure
the meaning of caresses given by a girl.

VERMIN

Sheep Tick
Fleas
Scabies
Lice

SHEEP TICK

I screamed the loudest if we found one:
a fat raised mole gorging off my shoulder.

'Where were you playing?' Mum moaned.
Dad just said it must have come off the animals.

(Our cat had ears like doylies
because of them)

Mum watched over my shoulder
while Dad chose the moment to dig,
swift, with his hard thumbnail.

She always told him
'Be sure and get its head out.'

I worried that they'd leave a tiny mouth and teeth
tunnelling inside me.

FLEAS

The black mark on my white vest
moved.

Half dressed I sat dumb with admiration
at its agility:
a standing start to infinity.

Then the beastie cracked between my mother's thumb-
nails.

All else I remember
is standing cold and naked
in a bath of ankle deep water.

My mother said if any were left
they'd jump.

SCABIES

When I became one huge burning itch
I rubbed and chewed and bit
till there was blood on the bedsheets.

I gnawed my hands at night
worrying between the fingers.

Our GP said my skin eruptions ran
in the family and prescribed
something for eczema.

Patiently Mum rubbed the stuff
into my most tender folded places.
The chemist suggested an old-fashioned remedy.

The bottle was made of thick brown glass
with fluted edges.

Each night I screamed it burned
and begged her to stop.

It tasted bad
so I couldn't chew my fingers.

I slept better then,
its stickiness gluing the pyjamas
to my heated skin.

LICE

'Hold still, keep out my light.
Something's moving.'

I sat frozen.
My wet washed hair dripped
waist length.

Startled sisters sat round watching.
We all held our breaths.

I wanted to cry.
That hair was my only glory.

Mum took a steel comb
and probed along my parting.

'In the name of God
she's got lice.'

I wasn't to tell anyone at school.

Next day I stayed indoors
head wrapped in a purple towel.
It smelled of something thick and sticky.
It made my scalp nip.

In the evening I combed out my hair
bowed over sheets of paper
and cremated the tiny bodies in the grate.

CATALOGUING MANUSCRIPTS

1.
You haven't lain long in the strongroom
among the other cardboard boxes
of literary remains.

The accessions register bears your epitaph:
Norman McLaren, letters to Florence Russell,
1936–86, a gift.

– all those confidences and passions preserved
for the nation;
humidity controlled, temperatures even.

I've to put your life together.
I exhume you at an office desk.

2.
Three British monarchs succeed each other
on the Canadian stamps you sent to a girl back home
at her four different Scottish addresses.

Over her shoulder I read
cuttings, postcards, articles, letters.
They chart the rise of a local boy making good
in the Commonwealth.

Not just my fingers feel grubby.

I'm uneasy reading letters
without my name in them.

3.
Gathering up tissue thin petals
I slip them back between the leaves
of a twenty year-old letter.

I file away gallery print postcards
and letters with illustrations in the margins.

A catalogue sent as a present shows
that a Chinese picture letter like these
hangs in Canada's National Art Collection.

4.
You say you're making good progress
but more and more letters are sent on
hospital crested paper.

I wish I could know that she sent back
all the right answers.

Eight months after you write of making a will
I try to put your papers in order.

LATE PERIOD

We just drank coffee and talked.

You rubbed my stomach
till acrylic blue sparks crackled off my jersey
then you joked that something kicked you.

There was one day left
till we'd know if I was reprieved.

Earlier that day I'd paced across the meadows
trying to shake my stomach free of that tight feeling
– cramps I was sure like any other month.

I lay down to bed
my eyes dry with tiredness.

With you gone the toy bear beside me
wouldn't give any comfort.

Six am: I need to pee.
The light bleaches my face grey
as it hangs in the mirror.

I put a foot on the bath edge
to open myself with my fingers
and search for flecks of blood.

VICTIM OF VIOLENCE

The police issued a statement.

There had been people in the area who must
have heard her screaming.
Please could they come forward.

My address near enough was given
as the scene of the crime.

I checked for details down the newspaper column.

Yes, I'd been at home.
If I had only known to lean from my window
I could almost have seen it happen.

Nightmares plagued me.

I lay below leadweight sheets trying to rise.
I couldn't reach you.
I didn't hear you.

I pass by the spot every day:
a pretty space of mown grass, flowerbeds,
now as silent as a well-kept grave

and I hear you screaming.

THE PICTURES

To avoid distracting the workers
the mill windows were set in the roof.

Consequently my mother never saw sense
in spending an evening in the cinema
with no air and not even light.

But she did go to see *Gone With The Wind*
when it first came out.

It was the same day Bessie Henderson's hair
caught in her loom and she was scalped.

The men came running
but they were no use, fainting and going on.

A woman had to hold Bessie up
while an engineer cut her loose.
The worst of it was she didn't faint.

Bessie should have been one of the girls
who went to see *Gone With The Wind*.

My mother tried
but she couldn't like it much.

PUBLIC LIBRARY ASSISTANT

A young man returns *Wedding Etiquette and Speech*
                                           Making
then requests something on ballroom dancing.

I understand these young girls
with their armfuls of paperback romances
but don't you wives get enough of the real thing?

Silent I wield my datestamp over *Infertility*
and *Coping with Bereavement*.

I note no improvements in the reader
who took out three aerobics books
and Wholefood Cookery.

I count the day's passage
as books are returned to dates
further down the counter.

In August keen schoolchildren descend
each with a booklist
chasing the same few volumes.

JANEY

My mother had a cousin, Janey.
She was raped when she was seven.
After that she didn't grow.

Relatives remember seeing her always sitting quiet
like a wee doll.

She never spoke to her father and brothers
and crossed to the other side
when they entered the room.

If a man approached her on the pavement
she turned back home.

Ann just had to laugh,
the number of times she was in trouble
for Janey not going to school.

'I've fourteen other bairns to care for.
I cannae be wi her a the time.'

What kind of work was there for a girl like Janey.
No one worried out loud but perhaps
she'd be better in some kind of home.

Janey died suddenly at sixteen
of Spanish flu.

'It's a happy release for her,' diagnosed the doctor
'He should have murdered her too.'

ANOREXIA

I knew she had already died to me
the day I introduced her to my sister.

As understanding dawned she blurted
'You mean she's your age?
I'd have sworn she was forty.'

Insect fragile
she had the air of a stilt walker.
Just a blob of body
on top of two grotesquely jointed legs.

My hopes rose each lunch-hour
but she brought excuses.

– I've already eaten.
– I'm keeping my sandwiches for later.

Or worse still
she might murder a biscuit in front of me
morsel by morsel.

Her eyes guttered.
Features collapsed beneath the insupportable
weight of skin.

One evening she sat at my fireplace
would drink only black coffee
and remarked that she felt the cold.

Even through two layers of clothes
I could make out bands of rib
where her breasts should have been.

Failed dieter in D cups,
dimpled at elbow, belly, thighs,
I gazed at the incarnation of all my dreams.

AN UGLY LOVER (tries to explain)

When you first claimed to love me
the shock had a violence
which thrilled through me.

Why should he think to say that?
but I have the nerve to question only your eyes
as I lie against you.

Nothing in me has been taught
to accept such a statement.

Believe me
I don't want to ignore you
but it would seem gall to reply.

Oh yes, I love you
but always I am wondering
what blow are you softening me for –

where will it fall?

ABSENCE

I don't have the confidence to be grasping.

Before there has never been any chance
that either he or my feelings
would be returned.

I have chafed at dead hopes
till they gave off bad humours
and I sickened.

Now I miss you gently.
Your absence throbs faintly all day
like a tender wound.

No great gash where my heart
was laid bare.

Gazing down the calendar
to one date set beside an asterisk I sigh
as if willpower could bring you back faster.

This ache is cautious but dares to trust
that my absence is noted too.

Myself
I am the only souvenir I have
of you.

These walls took no interest.
They turned a blind eye
to all that went on within them.

The air holds no pictures of you.
Only my tortured eyes can't let go
printing your image on everything.

I twist alone
in the aching space of a single bed
once crammed with the pair of us.

The mattress doesn't moan for you.

I can't let me forget
that we giggled as we made room
for my pushy breasts.

My skin harps on:
it can describe the entire length of you.

The sheets held only your scent.

REPOTTING A PLANT

This plant sulks,
a tensed green frown.

Obstinate
it sets its face to the light
rebels against narrow clay horizons.

Disconsolate
it lets a yellowed leaf drop.
No amount of water does.

Two days later
it lets itself droop again across its pot
chin in arms.

To look at you makes my feet ache
and think of tight shoes.

At last I act,
spread newspaper across the kitchen table,
fetch pebbles, compost, a larger tub.

Roots nose through the drainage holes;
I hear tears as I tug you loose,
unwrap those cruel Chinese bindings.

And there you sit exposed,
naked from the waist down.

BREAST EXAM

Every month I could find something wrong
if I wanted to
in that strange adipose tissue

– once I realised it was a rib
I'd been kneading.

Every month the same ritual:
arms raised before a mirror,
any marks, discharges dimples?

Familiar territory
but as difficult to read as a contour map
of the Himalayas.

Blue veins pulse on a white background
like dark rivers.

I lower my arms.
The slopes shift and settle.

On my left breast a faded scar
reminds me of the lesson I learned at fifteen.
It can't always happen to other people.

DIRTY WEEKEND

Foreplay begins at the station,
continues on the train.

Eyes at least can meet,
hands touch.

Later we play games in our shower en suite,
washing off our usual scents
of sex love sweat.

I mouth your shoulder and taste warm water,
your skin smooth as soap.

We are used to flatmates,
shared facilities.

Here we can wallow together
in our modest hired luxury.

Forty-eight hours to ourselves.
An entire weekend laps around us
as endless as the unaccustomed acres of double bed.

A SWIM

The Freedom
The Luxury
Horsing Around

THE FREEDOM

The short-sighted never need modesty
even in a communal changing room.

Bodyless voices din at me
floating over the cubicle curtain
rippling against the wet tiles.

– This swimsuit makes me fat.
– God, look at my stomach.

A bumless fifteen year-old blushes
as she slips a penny
into the weighing machine.

I strip off
confident that I am as blurred
as the bodies around me.

I'm too out of focus
to concentrate on cellulite, wrinkles, pot bellies.

I sashay from the shower room
an exhibitionist displaying cleavage, vaccination scars,
four pale bare limbs.

I who have never sported on a Summer beach
stride to the pool's edge
in turquoise lycra.

THE LUXURY

Someone else shines up these tiles,
picks the hair out the plug.

I stand with bowed head
beneath the steady stream of hot water
for as long as I like.

No fuel bills.
No door for anyone to bang on.

Only one little shock
– the cold blast of the disinfecting spray
on my hot water reddened feet.

Then I give myself up
to that massive bath.

My limbs lie outstretched.
I hang suspended on my back
like a huge rudderless starfish.

This is the life,
savouring the glide of the water,
soothing any strains, easing the aches.

Back in the showers
we have only ourselves to tend,
shampoos, conditioners, footprints left in talc.

HORSING AROUND

Going for a swim together
we're lucky if we make a length.

Here the laws of gravity end:
I'm a weightless nymph shrieking
as you lift my feet off the ground.

The lifeguard turns a blind eye
to passions kept cool
just below the surface.

Otterlike you skim beneath me;
a hanging island
wondering where you'll break for air.

Surprised
you discover that breasts float.

Among your chilled beard
I taste the warm shock of your mouth.

THE BED AND BREAKFASTS

They beamed into our lives
from nowhere –
one night stands on their Highland holidays.

Such exotica
when a carful arrived from America.

Enthroned in the sitting-room with the piano, best sofa,
the bed and breakfasts relished
fresh-laid eggs, homegrown vegetables.

My infantile craft,
hanging on the garden gate as they drove away,
was usually good for sixpence.

Only once
did anything come back to us
from their faraway imagined countries
– a packet of photos from Holland.

My sisters wear sensible shoes, print dresses.
I'm a toddler with hair curled like wood shavings.

Perhaps those children still smile from a Dutch album:
memories of a twenty years ago holiday?
quaint anthropological studies?

Less than a year later it all changed.
Dad worked in a factory,
we lived in a new town.

WOMAN WITH LILAC SASH

(Lady Agnew of Lochnaw *c.* 1893 by John Singer Sargent, 1856–1925)

Self composed Edwardian lady
you sit firm-backed in your period chair.

The broad silk sash winds twice
round a handspan whalebone waist
I don't envy you.

Forever at home to visitors
you keep it formal as we wander past.

You've held this pose for a century
fresh as yesterday
in your endless prime.

What did you think
during all those sittings?

Did convention bend
to let you chat with the artist?

Somewhere Madam
your chaperone still hovers
just outside the frame.

Dark eyes, cool brow,
every raven tress in its place,
you give away nothing but your loveliness.

THE LADIES WALDEGRAVE (by Joshua Reynolds)

(The girls' Uncle, Horace Walpole, said of the painting
– 'a most beautiful composition: the pictures are very
like and the attitudes natural and easy.')

Three little maids:
I can hear them chatter.

Once they had a governess,
worked cross-stitch onto samplers,
were visited by a dancing master.

They learned to play a little, sing a little,
paint silk screens
and speak some French.

Now they sit, accomplished young ladies
arranged to advantage
in harried seamstresses' dresses,
crowned by a wigmaker's craft.

They vie for suitors
whiling away the time together
on some useless article

pleasing compositions
of white lead, rouge and paint.

REVIEWED

I'm hot with embarrassment
reading this considered paragraph.

Inevitable it has loomed at me
ringed in my mind like obligatory
gym periods at high school.

It's the first time since PE
that I've been called
just my surname;

four grim syllables hurled the length of the pitch
where I floundered in mud,
face like a flushed turnip.

I'm exposed like my legs
as they mottled blue and red
on the hockey field.

A moment drenched in shame
as if I'd missed a catch,
fallen flat.

In the distance Mrs Turner bawls
'McSeveney, run it under a cold tap!'

CASTLE GUIDE

By the bus load
I gather cross sections of society
into my keeping.

In the next forty minutes
we'll spend four centuries together.

I discourse about the bed hangings
and the 5th Baronet's scandalous behaviour.

(nb never mention beds
to mixed school parties.)

Children fidget:
they're only here for the dungeons.

A boy scout peels paint
from the wall of the Blue Room.

Over coffee we pool our complaints:
sore feet, sore throats,
and all the same stupid questions.

The cleaner sighs as she polishes,
notes the fingerprints,
a small item pilfered.

By the end of the Season
I can bellow 'Don't touch'
in five different languages.

AN APPOINTMENT FROM THE MENTAL HOSPITAL

The information came in a discreet
brown paper wrapper.

There was a strict code of practise:
no miracle cures were promised,
no embarrassing catalogues would follow.

There were the usual terse details:
day place and doctor.

Our business was strictly confidential
carried on privately in public.
There was no return address on the envelope.
I opened it alone in secret.

For once I did bear pain without complaining.
I wouldn't expect encouragement or comfort
when it was all in my mind.

PREJUDICES

I've heard stories...
girls locked up for life because
they'd had illegitimate babies

and jokes about generators
and rubber mattresses.

Scared stiff
I consider the idea of delivering myself
into that sort of keeping.

Mad:
I'll never hold down a job,
be a loyal friend, a good mother.

Walking towards the hospital.
I see nurses airing the long-term patients.

There's an old old lady,
wrinkled socks, fallen chest,
a dress made of apron material.

It's too late.
Already somewhere there's a cabinet
with my file in it.

AT THE SHRINK

The camp part of me wants a couch
to lie on but he offers
only an easy chair.

I try to settle down in it.

I can hear the whisper of his pencil
against the paper
as he jots down notes.

The point jerks like a seismograph
measuring the impact of my answers.

I blurt out some startling truth
and watch, baffled,
when his right hand doesn't move.

VIVISECTION

he works without anaesthetic

his questions
have a fine cutting edge
peeling back layer after layer

impassive
when the pain takes my breath
away

I am braced
for each shock

witchpricker
he never finds a spot
that doesn't hurt

laid open
I spill my guts

GONE WRONG

I no longer fear reproaches
from family, teachers, friends.

I remember running amok
screaming till my voice split
but what could I expect?

I wasn't well then.

But in the back of my mind
a child persists.
'Don't blame me,' she says.

Her handwriting is in my old books.
Her teddy is beside my bed.
I have her ponytail in a plastic bag.

I see her robustly ordinary
skipping in a schoolyard.

'It's not my fault,' she claims.
'I read the Famous Five, kept pets,
believed in Santa Claus.'

What are you doing Woman?
I've been a disappointment in you.

SMEAR TEST

Left in the cubicle to my own devices
I examine the speculum.
It's bigger than I thought.

I fold towelling underwear
on top of a white petticoat
on top of canvas shoes.

It's Summer:
each waistband is sweatdamp.

Nothing else for it,
I take off my body
and arrange it on the couch.

The doctor apologises that I had to wait,
warms the speculum under a hot tap.
I am not afraid. We chat.

Prepared for the next virginal loss
I give myself up to the first touch
of medical steel.

UNDER FIVE

The potato drills ran out at my horizon.

There was a white hen with one eye.
She followed me like a dog
and lived on because I loved her.

One day the sky exploded.
I screamed for help at the barn door
battered blind by hailstones.

Under the rhododendron bush
I came face to face with a thundering bee
big as my staring eyeballs.

One night the grass turned white and brittle.
I rolled all over it
in an empty meal sack.

Likewise those Northern sunsets
baffled me.

My mother wore Summer dresses
with the wide polka dot skirts
now back in fashion.

MOLE

I disliked the thing for years
warned not to scratch myself
in case I made it grow or bleed.

Squinting backwards into a mirror
I saw a brown blob reflecting distantly
like a brand.

The distinguishing signature
on a broad pale canvas
it gave me the creeps.

Years later I'm at my GP.
She takes too much interest in this mark
I can hardly see.

Is it a joke?
as I'm measured with a twelve inch ruler,
asked about size shape colour.

Childhood nightmares of it seeping everywhere
like a vast dark stain
are partly coming true.

Just to be on the safe side
it ought to be removed.

Sense stops my protests
but I'm amazed that any part of me
can be erased like pencil marks from paper.

Again I gaze over my shoulder
at the dark raised strawberry
so long a hallmark of me.

BOUQUET

He brought me roses unexpectedly
on our third date
because it was my birthday I thought.

He dropped the knot into my lap casually;
a posy from his garden,
handpicked, the stems bound in tin foil.

There was a full headed red,
three yellows just budding,
one white curled like a soft shell.

Real roses:
thorns, patches of rust,
leathery leaves pocked by insects
and ohh that scent.

I stood them in a glass
at the corner of my bedroom.

In that heavy Summer night
the petals parted without a sound and let go
such a perfume from their discreet pores.

By morning the room
was sweet with it,
the first red petals scattered on the floor.

BACK INJURY

I could spit
to think that only weeks ago I could
hop from bed, pull back the curtains.

All with this same body
unappreciated, ticking over,
in good order.

Today I give myself
a half hour's pep talk before I dare try
easing myself from the horizontal.

FUCK!

My eyes stream with frustration
as I try to dress without bending.

Already I feel in part defeated:
all my good humour gone
and not even out of the bedroom.

The day twists ahead
bristling with obstacles.

Planning every footstep
the bathroom next door might as well
be a mile away.

MUSCLE SPASM

Suddenly
a hidden fist grabs a handful
of me.

I tell my torso I would like
to bend forward.

The spirit is yelling that it's willing
but the flesh, stiff as a board,
won't give an inch.

My left foot doesn't care a hoot
about straight lines:
puts a little twist into every step.

Like a crazed marionette
I am jangling in all
directions

my strings
tangled
in a strange hand.

PHYSIOTHERAPIST

First I must stand in my underwear
as hugely visible as if raised on a plinth.
My only diagnosis: it hurts.

She walks round me
like one of those artgazers
who circle every statue
plant themselves before each canvas
while my eyes flit about
ignorant.

Never have I been so thoroughly observed.

We get me onto a couch.
My embarrassed skin sticks to the leather
with a squeak.

Am I still clean enough?

She explains:
pain has pushed me out of kilter
for so many months that now
(even when I think I have)
I don't straighten up.

I experiment
and she's right.
Standing fair and square my pelvis,
nudged aside, still tilts.

Hard to credit:
all this time it's the misdirected power
of my own body
that has held me in check.

THE SECOND-HAND DRESS

I zip myself into curves as deep
as Sophia Loren's
in a boned swimsuit,

pat myself into a ruched bosom
which is pure Liz Taylor
giving it hell in Tennessee Williams.

Circa 1958 someone wore this
next to her figure of eight frame
like a second skin.

She still haunts the print cotton
as I wear her old dress among crowds
of Doc Martens and black leggings.

My flat sandals want to click.
I feel my three and a half feet
of unrepentant hips start to sway.

But she's shaking her head at my liberated
unwaxed unstockinged legs,
no gloves, no shampoo and set.

I was born too late.
Three inches too small in the bust
I can't fill this woman's place.

WINDOWBOX

I sowed nightscented stocks with the halfgrown hope
that this was more like gardening
than impatiens in pots.

They grew anaemic and spindly
coated by dust from the street.
From the ground they looked like weeds.

Nothing flashy or flowery
like a trumpetting hippaestrum
or a petal drenched Black-eyed Susan

and even I who planted them
rarely thought to look out
except maybe in the evenings

when the cool damp of Summer rain
sweated in the air
like an extra sense

and the night scent swam in
clear as spearmint
and soothed away the city noise.

Then there grew a garden:
rosebeds and herbs,
tangles of scarlet runners.

FRIENDSHIP CAKE

She's less bother than a pet,
keeps quiet in a plastic bowl
on a corner of the sideboard.

She doesn't ask for much

happy to scavenge on soured milk,
eggs past their sell by date,
any kind of cooking oil.

Every five days or so
I chuck in more ingredients,
give her a stir, knock out the lumps,

and she settles down again to gestate
under a clean teacloth.

She gives the kitchen a productive smell
as she belches little bubbles
digesting steadily,
working on her yeasty alchemy.

LANGUAGE SCHOOL: REGISTERING FOR A CLASS

I sit across from a tutor
who is expecting me to speak
in the language of my choice.

I'm appalled:
she really is French
and still she is expecting me to speak.

I am struck both dumb
and reckless
with embarrassment.

I have to explain.
I don't need to discuss life or politics
just entrance fees and postcard prices,
give tourists directions to the nearest bank.

Now for the dreadful initiation.
I stammer something
launch at her my wild conjugations.

From the other desks
I catch phrases of Spanish, Japanese, German
like some linguistic karaoke night.

THREE HAIKU

a spider plant climbs
across a big paper moon:
my neighbour's window

Edinburgh
in winter; the McEwan Hall
dreams of Italy

my niece draws a place
where the tulips grow four feet high:
must be Paradise

PONYTAIL

My old ponytail lies curled in a top drawer
among the usual clutter
of scarves and purses and combs.

It's kept neat in the same plastic bag
that the hairdresser put it in
on that first trip to her salon.

The baptismal snips
grated at the nape of my neck.

She gathered up handfuls
like she was stooking hay
and put it aside for me.

For a few years I could still detect
the medicated scent of dandruff shampoo
but now it smells of polythene.

I take it out from time to time
and I'm always amazed
by how alive it is.

It's never aged or withered or faded.

Far more vivid evidence than family snaps
or formal school portraits
that I once existed aged twelve.

I'm going grey now,
have hints of varicose veins, dropped breasts,
a dodgy back.

But the ponytail is still glossy.
It never lost its colour or bounce,
still has the auburn highlights my mother loved.